Avenue Claude Vignon, French Riviera.

Sketching and Painting
OUT OF DOORS

---

written and illustrated by
ADRIAN HILL
V.P.R.B.A., R.O.I.

LONDON
BLANDFORD PRESS

First published 1961
Second impression 1963

167 High Holborn, London WC1

For
BARBARA AND ROLANDS COLDICOTT

Printed in Great Britain by
Jarrold and Sons Ltd, Norwich

Contents

List of Illustrations

IN COLOUR

IN BLACK AND WHITE

Adrian Hill

Introduction

"THE artist . . . is also a born adventurer. His explorations, unlike those of the tourist, are rewarded by the discovery of beauty spots unmentioned in the guide books, and with tireless curiosity and an exceptional proneness to wonderment, he will come upon objects of remarkable interest overlooked or even shunned by more disciplined observers."

These wise words by Augustus John, R.A., could not be bettered to introduce and support the claims which are hopefully submitted in the following chapters.

There are, of course, many professional painters whose landscapes in current art shows do not bear any clear record of having been painted out of doors and which in some cases do not have much resemblance to Nature's form of colouring. But this is not to say that these artists do not paint direct from Nature, or have not done so in the past—and with diligence. I would say further that it is only when the artist paints on the spot that he has a real inspiration born of the integrity of a personal vision.

The reader may therefore dismiss any doubt that may linger in his mind as to whether out-door painting is not somewhat out of date and not worth the trouble it entails.

Since many books have already been published on this subject from the purely technical standpoint, I have tried to enlarge on several factors generally considered as ancillary but which, in my experience, merit more than a passing reference.

Painting out of doors is a very human pursuit which can at times produce violent reactions of discomfort, vexation and frustration. These feelings must be expected and accepted if the joy of achievement is to be attained.

So much depends, surely, on what we hope to *get out of Nature*; to realise our hopes we have to *get into Nature*—and the sooner we do so, the better!

A pencil drawing of Ipswich Docks.

A detailed drawing of a street in Paris, where the heavy cast shadow enhances the composition.

1 *The Sketch and the Sketch Book*

THIS little book is not addressed to the complete beginner, but to the reader who can draw with a certain proficiency and has already practised the techniques of oil or watercolour painting.

No student of painting, however much progress he has made, can be said to have experienced all the excitement and enjoyment there is if he has shrunk from the adventure of working out of doors. Without doubt it needs courage and an undaunted will to succeed in the face of the numerous little hazards involved in its practice. Nevertheless the serious student who has hitherto been content "to ride at anchor" in the safe harbour of his own studio and who has never had the courage "to hoist his sails and venture to meet the elements outside"—if such a nautical simile is allowed—is refusing one of the most valuable gifts that Nature has to offer. Knowledge and subject matter which are culled from memory or second-hand sources lack true pictorial nourishment which can only be gathered and garnered direct from Nature's storehouse—to change the metaphor.

As the title of this book suggests, there is a difference between sketching and painting when the two are practised out of doors. While sketching does not imply making a picture, painting can and often does suffice for a completed statement which can be framed and exhibited—and even sold!

This sketch and the one opposite are examples of working drawings, squared up, for subsequent pictures which were painted away from the subject. As can be seen, they are done without regard for style, but contain everything necessary for composition and detail.

Let us take the sketch first.

Now a sketch can be something done for the joy of it—complete in itself, slight and swiftly executed, and judged on these merits. It can also remain, and often does, as a part of a picture, a detailed portion for some larger work. It can apply to what I would call an investigation into something that interests one for itself alone, or as a possible future reference. And it can be a working rough for a definite picture—a "try out"—a way of finding out what the potential pictorial value of the scene is. In this case the initial sketch is developed into a definite working drawing, which can be squared up and followed faithfully in the larger painting.

All these forms of sketching have their proper place in our art life (as well as training), to be produced (when necessary, as a testimony of our study) in our sketch books. Such books, in an increasing variety of sizes and surfaces of paper, can be obtained from any artists' colourman, together with a wide range of pencils, chalks or crayons. Indeed, you can travel far and collect a vast amount of useful reference with a couple of sketch books, 6 in. by 8 in. and 14 in. by 10 in., and a box of pencils or crayons —or both!

In the body of this book I have introduced examples of what I hope covers nearly all the different ways of sketching—except with charcoal, a lovely descriptive instrument, but lacking the stuff or substance for making solid studies which will not rub or smudge, remaining as precise as when first drawn.

Five-minute sketch of Brighton Pier, seen from a high viewpoint.

HOW TO USE A SKETCH BOOK

These examples from my own sketch books will cover much of the ground. They have been executed as a working artist in various parts of the country and abroad over a number of years. The reader can therefore trace for himself any sign of improvement and agree or not with choice of matter and style and general worthwhileness of the evidence produced. Many of the studies have remained for years hidden away in drawers; others have been destroyed; but quite a number have proved very useful as working drawings for a painting, either as a whole or in supplying authentic detail in a large composition. In the doing of them all, I consider I added more knowledge and authority to my job as a painter; in all of them I learnt something more about the things I drew; and in all of them, whatever merit they possess, I found enjoyment—real enjoyment in the concentrated effort which such study demands.

Painstaking study of farm machinery in lead-pencil (3B). Notice regard for light and shade.

From experience, I would advise the would-be artist: don't give up drawing because you find it difficult, and if sketching comes easy to your hand, don't be satisfied with a facile style but regard your drawing in the light of investigation: the deeper you probe, the more you will discover. Clever superficial drawings, like smart repartee, suffer from repetition.

Naturally personal preferences are revealed in the choice of certain aspects of the countryside, that is inevitable, but I have always tried to heed the warning that nobody draws well who only draws one kind of subject, or object. I have often purposely turned my attention to the portrayal of scenes which I knew to be generally outside the range of my scope or pictorial interests.

This self-discipline, may I add, has proved salutary when commissions with unfamiliar subject matter have come along. I believe that in the last analysis the sketch book will always prove to be the artist's best friend. *Develop the sketch book habit!*

I should just add that drawings such as these, in which essential detail is included, to be of future use should be sprayed with fixative—especially if they are executed in crayon, conte or carbon pencil. The continued pressure of the sheets of paper upon each other with the repeated turning of the leaves of a sketch book can be very detrimental to the freshness and clarity of studies done in any graphic medium, except of course the pen.

(above) *Barges at Port Sunlight. Drawing, tinted with coloured crayons.*

(below) *Low Tide at Tower Bridge. Carbon pencil and tint.*

Pen drawing over pencil outline.

2 *With Pen and Ink and Wash*

SKETCHING from Nature direct with a pen will be found to be a mixed blessing. Its directness is half its charm, for anything, whether it be a single object or a view, that is drawn so that it stands or falls without alteration, has a claim on our respect, envy, admiration or tolerance, according to the degree of its success. But with a technique of such swift finality it is often doubtful evidence of the actual object or scene it purports to describe.

Does this matter? Artistically, no. It depends on what future use you may have for the drawing. As an exercise to increase confidence in handling, as a means of demonstrating spontaneous enjoyment of the thing seen, or as an antidote to an over-careful and laboured approach to the subject, a pen, or better still, fountain pen with an easy flow of Indian ink, is a wonderfully

A fine line pen drawing emphasising the character of the buildings and boats.

A pen drawing where tone is used to give mass effect, as well as detail.

expressive instrument, but not, I think, an instrument of exact truth. It can exaggerate beautifully, it can transform (or disfigure) according to the tractability or transmutability of the touch. With a pen you may, to misquote the poet, "intend an ode and produce a sonnet!" By the exact truth, I mean that if, for example, the slant of your tree is off the mark, if the intervals between one form and another are too wide or too narrow, or their proportion one to another is out of scale, the sketch, while appealing to the fresh, extempore manner of its communication and containing the excitement of an impulsive impression, may prove of little value as a *working drawing* for future picture making.

Having said that, it must be emphasised that drawing with a pen or any instrument which cannot be erased or altered, quite apart from the exciting results which are the reward for such courage, will improve your technical ability to master the job. A lack of precision is unavoidable and forgiveable, especially in the early stages.

It may well be that a desire to combine accuracy and spontaneity with the pen will prompt a compromise by which you ink over the lines of a pencil drawing, but if you look at the illustrations on page 16 I think you will notice a lack of freshness in those that have been done this way.

Washes of sepia to augment the pen line can be used where shadows and depth are wanted. Such a mixture has found favour with graphic artists down the ages and can lend pictorial truth to a topographical scene.

In the following chapter I will be discussing this type of subject recording for the sketch book.

3 *The Topographical Sketch*

I HAVE always retained an abiding affection and admiration for the topographical drawing done on the spot. Attempts to emulate the graphic masters in this particular and exacting genre continually appear in my early sketch books. Their origin, I suppose, can be traced back to my appointment as a war artist, when for nearly two years I concentrated on recording the ruins of the French village, town and countryside, as the devastating hand of war laid them waste. Although under the ruthless demolition of artillery and air bombardment, in my terms of reference a certain degree of accuracy was vitally necessary in recording how they stood the shock, and in what order of ruination they still preserved their personality and locality. Herein lay the foundation of speed and truth in presentation, which I laboured so conscientiously to perfect. While it was a directive in those far off days, it has remained a challenge ever since.

Only recently, I found a reproduction of a drawing by John Ruskin (1819–1900) of the Palazzo Contarine-Fasan in Venice, which rekindled my respect for the skill of tackling such a subject and giving pictorial verisimilitude to the detailed façade of these over-ornamented Italian buildings, *and in perspective* too! For I need not remind you that Ruskin was only an amateur, and if he could do it, why shouldn't the reader try his hand at recording with accuracy such subjects where architecture takes pride of place?

(With the permission of the Imperial War Museum, Kenningto

Pen and wash drawing of Peronne, France, 1918.

I know this accurate portrayal of Nature is respected by some modern schools of thought only as a relic of past virtuosity, but the fact remains that these reminders of how both professional and amateurs tackled Nature should make us query the wisdom of turning our backs completely on the topographical sketch. Indeed, I believe I detected a shade of envy when a young contemporary painter said to me recently, "I don't suppose I could do it, if I tried, but then why should I, for who wants it anyhow?" I was inclined to agree with the first part of his statement, but I believe there is a growing desire for a return to the skill and craft

A topographical sketch where detail is concentrated in the drawing of the tow

BAZAR
PROMENAD
SUZE

which such accuracy of representation demands. After all, such masters of sketching as Turner, a veritable magician with pencil or pen, Gainsborough, Constable, Guitin, Cotman and James Stark—to mention only a few names that immediately spring to the mind—could all combine exactitude with an emotive notation, and they all remain "living" painters.

Surely the sketch books of the past should re-awaken the desire to continue this time-honoured practice and experience the thrill which comes from an eager recognition of the exact spot or locality when your sketch comes under review.

A faithful drawing of one of five Land Gates at Bruges in Belgium.

4 *Oil Painting*

THERE are a number of professional painters who are able to paint up to a 36 in. by 28 in. oil (and perhaps even larger) on the spot. The confidence and control necessary for this feat is developed only after many years of practice and mastery over one's tools in the face of all kinds of weather conditions. This is a claim which few of us can make, and readers who aim at such proficiency in out-door painting must devote many years of dogged study before anything like a successful painting on this scale is achieved.

I find that a 24 in. by 20 in. is an ideal size which can be comfortably controlled, and "control" is the operative word! On the rare occasions when I have tackled anything over a 30 in. by 25 in., I have seen to it that the conditions have been as perfect as nature and the close proximity of a house or shelter can provide!

To begin with, I recommend 14 in. by 10 in. or 16 in. by 12 in. as good sizes. Sizes smaller than this, if always used, will limit your subject matter and cramp your style. You will in any event be sitting at a sketching easel which should offer you plenty of arm movement and keep you at the right distance from your painting.

Painting boards, of which there are a great variety, are preferable to canvas on a stretcher, being more portable, but I find that wood panels (which are often included in the furnishing of an oil box) are too absorbent, unless primed and first given a coat of flat white. Oiled paper, which you can buy by the sheet and cut to any size you want, is cheap and serviceable but has not sufficient substance for exhibition work and is apt to tear under excessive weight of paint. It also necessitates a board on which to pin it. Canvas boards are, I suppose, the most popular.

If you use only turps as a medium, you will find that your painting dries very quickly, a point to remember when packing up to return home.

While drawing can often be done standing up, or sitting on the ground, a light folding canvas-covered stool is indispensable for painting in oils. Such a stool, made of aluminium, can be carried over the arm and is no encumbrance on your journey out and back. The leather seated tripod design, while appearing more substantial, is awkward to carry, heavy in comparison and in my experience slightly insecure on uneven ground.

There are many designs of light folding easels on the market. The chief thing to remember in making your choice is that it must be easy to erect, secure when standing and quickly folded up. The easel which has too many gadgets is generally a puzzle to open out and sometimes collapses without warning!

A well-made canvas satchel, large enough to contain your colours, brushes, rags, palette and turps, and carried over your shoulder by a stout leather strap, can obviate the purchase of a more expensive painting box, carried by hand, which can become very heavy.

So far I have envisaged the reader with no other means of transport than that provided by his own two legs. With a car, of course, it is a very different and simpler matter, as all you have to do is to see you have everything you want safely deposited in the boot. For those then who own a car, I can leave the subject of equipment without further comment. I will just add, for the pedestrian, that a metal device, with handle, for clamping two wet

Garden sketch in oils. The strip of sky, background wall and hedge were painted in that order. An example of working forward to the immediate foreground. Time: 1 hour.

The Water Mill, Lacock, Wiltshire. Painted and completed in oils on the spot in a sitting of three hours. Size 30 × 25.

paintings face to face without touching, is on the market and is obviously essential if no transport is available.

I have seen photographs of Sir Winston Churchill, painting at ease, in great comfort under the shelter of a vast painting umbrella—but we lesser mortals, can and mostly must, dispense with such luxury! Shade can generally be found, even if it means sitting in the shadow of your car.

In passing, painting on a small scale can just be done inside a car, but movement and visibility are very restricted. Small water-colours are about all I can manage, and I do it only if the weather makes it impossible to venture out. Indeed it seems almost like cheating to get round "the rigours of the game", as Charles Lamb would, I am sure, have described painting out of doors.

(At the Municipal Art Gallery, Oldham.)

Oil paintings completed on the spot in three hours. Size 24 × 20.

(In the possession of R. T. Phillips.)

An Early Spring Subject

5 *An Early Spring Subject*

BEFORE the trees actually burst into leaf, there is a pregnant period at the end of March and the beginning of April when woods and spinneys, thickets and hedgerows are seen to be mantled in a veiling of transparent tints of colour difficult to name, chromatically elusive—warm amber?—honey?—russet? The actual hue is as transient as the passing scent of the Scots Pine, which ever evades a savouring to the full. It is Nature's swift prelude or string overture to the richer orchestration of the Four Seasons' Opera to follow, and a challenge to the painter to venture out with his paints rather than with a sketch book and pencil.

The example I have chosen to illustrate some of the problems involved in this endeavour is in no way presented as anything but an honest-to-goodness study; its only value is in what can be learnt about Nature's behaviour at this phase of her development. It was executed in oils, under a changeable sky with a variable wind and under a threat of rain!

I was chiefly concerned with the problem of sky and distance, as the branches of the three foreground trees only permitted glimpses of the former. As will be seen, they form a lattice work, between the intervals of which the painting of the sky would have been laborious and the result very patchy. So I painted the sky all over and down to the silhouette of the distant trees, relying on my drawing direct with my brush when it came to painting the trees against (and over) the sky. Indeed, whenever more than one tree is outlined against the sky (except when in full summer the density of foliage precludes no more than small glimpses of the sky), this procedure of painting in the tree afterwards is the only logical one.

With the sky completed (and for this area the pigment should not be too lavishly applied but thinned out with turps), I proceeded with the background, using less medium and more actual paint, and taking care to keep my colours cool to render distance and atmosphere. The foreground I brushed in with raw sienna and a touch of Prussian blue and light red. This was to give a foundation to build up on and to cover up the white surface of my board.

Now I could tackle my three trees. With a largish brush (because the trees all possessed thick trunks), well loaded with a mixture of umber, light red, and a touch of viridian, I boldly built them *up from the bole*, sweeping my brush upwards in the direction of growth and taking care to follow the reduction of girth as they ascended into the sky area.

All three tree trunks were painted like this. Then with a small brush and more turps than before, I boldly swept in the branch formation, painting each bough and branch *away* from the parent trunk, so as to preserve their way of growth. I need hardly add that I did not attempt to paint all the branches, but only those that gave me the suggested form of the dry tree. (Neither in drawing nor painting a tree is it wise to attempt anything except an approximation of branch construction.)

The local colour of each tree trunk was then introduced—thickening perhaps a lower bough and generally attempting to lend a chestnut personality to what would otherwise have been "just trees".

Lastly the foreground was painted into the warm broken tints already brushed in. The final touches of white, suggestive I hoped of the distant grazing sheep, were introduced to act as a focal point of interest and break up the expanse of meadow between the two trees. As with the branches, I strictly rationed my number of sheep, which were actually dotted all over the middle distance for any attempt at a faithful recording would have produced a confusion of meaningless white spots.

Detail from An Early Spring Subject
(See page 32)

6 *Watercolours*

PAINTING out of doors in watercolours offers different rewards and presents other technical problems. With regard to equipment, while an easel makes for added ease when painting a watercolour of 22 in. by 15 in., it can be dispensed with when sketching on a smaller scale. By nursing your block on your knees you can, with practice, carry your colour box and palette on your thumb and with your free fingers hold your picture in position. In this case your water container is attached to the edge of your box. If your stool is low enough, you can rest your box and water jar on the ground beside you and, by bending over, mix your colours and make your washes with greater freedom. For painting out of doors I prefer tubes of paint to pans, as being moist they are more easily and quickly worked, and time, as we shall see, is a great factor.

The rewards are obvious to any admirer of this typically British way of painting. It is an exacting but perfect medium to depict the atmospheric effects under which our countryside is generally seen and enjoyed. To be of any practical value, advice can only stem from personal experience, and I am still persuaded that the watercolour which is completed in one sitting is the most satisfactory. It has always proved fatal to me to stop operations and continue later, even if the break is of short duration, and especially if the painting is taken up after a day's interval. The original drive and the fresh 'eye' are impossible to recapture, while second thoughts will be found—and bound—to suggest adjustments, improvements and even some drastic overhaul, which, however skilfully they are undertaken, will weaken the original zest and rob the handling of its pristine freshness.

This does not mean a slapdash technique, a hit or miss, or any evasion of the problems, but it does imply that however long or protracted the initial sitting is (and it can easily continue for a whole morning or afternoon), the painting will be executed in one steady concentrated effort and so preserve a continuity of handling. Moreover, I have always held that the lasting charm of a watercolour direct from Nature comes from an absence of labour (or obvious labour). It must flow without apparent interruption, but flow it must, for the rhythm will surely be broken if the stream of thought is held up in the course of its journey.

Any size up to 22 in. by 15 in. can be controlled with practice in one sitting, unless the preliminary drawing is a slow business, which I know is often the case, even with those up to professional standard. Once this hurdle is overcome, the painting should be swift and sure. Of course the actual speed of execution will depend on your ability and to a large extent on the nature and scope of your subject.

If a small impression of a simple view with straightforward lighting is all that is desired, it may only take fifteen minutes or so of visual and physical concentration to achieve the required result. If not, if by that time the sparkle is wearing off or the clarity of colour has been lost by overpainting, it is far better to stop, have a pause, and start the race over again. For a race it is, and always will be.

Generally speaking, then, the aim should be to make a completed statement, though it may be as economical in technique as a telegram message is in choice of words.

It is natural for the beginner to waste precious minutes fumbling with the mixing of the right tint, or failing to mix up a big enough wash to cover the required area, or (as so often is the case) to refrain from using a big brush which would do the job in one stroke, instead of several far less effectual ones with a smaller one. All these hesitations and vacillations impede the performance and waste time, but with practice and boldness they are mastered and then by instinct the hand will go as the eye dictates straight to the right colour and to the right size of brush. But this co-ordination will not be achieved unless the student recognises the value implicit in many failures, for in my experience it is only through the paintings that don't "come off" that there arrives at last the painting that does!

Now what sort of standard should we aim at?

I have recently inspected with interest and surprise many delightful watercolours handed down in Victorian sketch books. They all have a tender charm in their pictorial solicitude for Nature in design, colour and sentiment, and though circumspect in their period technical convention, they retain an artistic rectitude which demands respect. They contain both botanical truth and—despite their modest size—a feeling for grandeur. But though we may accept their myopic excellence, they act as a warning against small-scale exercises. The danger of looking only for certain picturesque aspects of Nature and painting them all the same size, and in the same style, is that though they may be sensitive in approach and are always faithful as records, this can only lead to pictorial stagnation.

The moral to be drawn is to keep your sketch books for pencil or chalk and use a sketching block for your paintings; in short, paint as large as you dare, rather than as small as safety dictates. Elbow room is what we want. To paint always in a sketch book must cramp the vision as well as the hand. If a strong or dramatic effect is required, it is far easier to draw in your subject boldly with chalk, on a board or a largish sketching block, than within the restricted boundaries of a sketch book. And see that your subsequent washes of colour stand up to, or even cancel out, these firm scaffolding lines.

I am reminded of the lovely limpid watercolours of later date by such experts as Wilson Steer and Pitchforth, which appear to have no scaffolding and are the admiration and envy of many who aspire to such feats of virtuosity. While it is only human to be fascinated by the magic of a master of technique, it has been rightly said, "Fortunately an artist's vision is his own and no one can borrow his eyes or his soul, though they may well nigh take the brush from his hand."

Mention of imitation should remind one of what John Ruskin wrote about imitation of Nature. "The chalk outline of the bough of a tree on paper is not an imitation, it looks like chalk and paper —not like wood, and that which it suggests to the mind is not properly said to be *like* the form of a bough, it *is* the form of a bough." "Imitation," he continues, "though producing the pleasure of surprise has no place in producing works of art." And somewhere else—I quote from memory—he warns his reader that while an artist can imitate a fruit but not a tree—so he can imitate a flower but not a pasture—cut glass but not a rainbow.

Such wisdom comes as a solace when we attempt to paint Nature *exactly as she is*, especially in terms of pure watercolour!

7 *Weather and Seasonal Problems*

IT is obviously far pleasanter to paint out of doors during the (we hope) settled summer months than in the early spring, late autumn or winter, when the vagaries and severities of the weather can play havoc with personal comfort and sometimes ruin any hopes of a finished painting. Any professional painter will endorse this, but he will also affirm with equal conviction that high summer often cannot compare with any of the preceding or following months for colour, tone and quality of the landscape.

Trees in high summer, especially in July and August, suffer from a monotonous colouration, and an all-over blue sky devoid of clouds lacks that element of movement and design so noticeable when the breezes of spring and the winds of autumn stir the countryside into a more lively painter's picture, and quicken the desire to record, however briefly, some impression of Nature in such exciting and vigorous moods. I am not implying that Nature is paintable only under such conditions—that would be absurd—but I am warning the reader that when the barometer stands at "set fair" the countryside does not always display to full advantage her pictorial potentialities as she does when the weather is "cloudy" or "unsettled". In other words, "bright intervals" or even "occasional showers" often offer a richer reward than when "settled weather" is forecast.

There is much to be said also for a grey day for offering the

The stark silhouette reflected in the flooded field is heightened by the quiet sky and high skyline.

outdoor painter a steady light in which the subject can be closely analysed without the tonal changes consequent on the fluctuating light and shade from a bright but cloudy sky. Such days we endure in plenty and although they do not promise exciting results, certain aspects of our countryside, in which interesting subject matter occurs, are made even more pictorially significant under an invariable light than when the subject is lost and found as the sun and shadows play tip and run all over the scene.

Naturally, on such days the sky portions should not occupy much of our picture area; in fact the paintings should be designed on the principle of the high horizon line and of a closed or intimate aspect of nature rather than of an open view.

So often we tackle the right subject under the wrong conditions and vice versa. The more we work out of doors the more we

Sunset After Rain, West Wittering, Sussex. A watercolour painted at speed and very wet to capture the passing sky effect.

Everything here was sacrificed in order to try to capture the swift departing glory of a sunset at Itchinor. An example of palette knife painting.

will find that there is time and place for the grave as well as the gay. The moods of Nature are many, and it is our job to choose so that whether she smiles or frowns on the scene it is presented in its right colours and under the most acceptable conditions. A leaden sky can heighten the silhouette of the forms of Nature outlined against it, just as a cloudy sky can soften the starkness and angularity of an industrial subject. Indeed the minor key for the eye as for the ear in music is often more enjoyable than the major one.

In the early stages, however, to paint without fear of sudden squalls of wind or rain or both gives an added feeling of confidence when tackling the problem of studying Nature at first hand. Fortunately there are plenty of subjects to be found that even favour the steady light from a clear or grey sky. Street, farm and harbour scenes can all be recommended, for here what is happening on the ground or in the water is of chief importance. Farm

The highlights on the tree trunks are contrasted against the soft shadows of the middle distance.

buildings, boat sheds, stable yards, offer the student excellent compositions, to which he can return for as many sittings as he thinks necessary for the completion of his picture. He must always bear in mind that his successive paintings must be made during the same period of the day, otherwise changing light and changing shadows will confuse the issue and wreck colour harmony.

So that full advantage can be taken when looking for a subject, it is advisable always to have your sketch book with you. It often happens in my experience that on the return journey some useful reference springs suddenly to the eye. It may only be a neglected piece of agricultural machinery or a disused boat waist high in a tangle of weeds or water (both common sights, by the way), or some farm cart standing on the verge of the road or against a hay-stack, fence or wall. Whatever its composition, the various shapes and local colour (which you can write in) will often provide

Study of farm cart for future reference.

A grey day study of farm buildings.

authentic additional "props" for some future paintings, lacking which a certain emptiness might be difficult to fill from memory.

An impish breeze or a sudden shower of rain, while sadly interfering with your work (and is quite disastrous to a wet watercolour wash), may force one to seek shelter, from which another view can fully compensate for the incompleteness of the interrupted study.

And if the worst comes to the worst and conditions make it impossible to continue painting, you can still use your eyes. Visual concentration on what is happening to change the colour and tone of the scene (as you plod home!) will show you how rain banishes shadows and at the same time dramatises lights on all horizontal planes, like flat surfaces of roads, tops of walls and slanting roofs. It can also be seen to "rub out" all reflections in a pond or river, effectually rob the middle distance of detail and often obscure the horizon completely.

The contrast is made more apparent at the moment when the weather breaks and the watery sun makes its shy appearance to galvanise the landscape afresh, adorning it with iridescent colours, the light of which now awakens its obedient shadows, temporarily obscuring and revealing form and contour as they follow in swift attendance over the sparkling prospect. It is then, surely, that we realise what a quick-change artist Nature can be, and how many faces she has!

A composition where weather and light play little part.

8 *Companion and Audience*

SKETCHING out of doors in company, especially with one whose work you admire, can give a sense of unfair competition and a decided inferiority complex when studies are compared. On the other hand, to go out with one of your own experience and ability adds zest to your own painting, and gives moral support when the unwanted passer-by lingers too long in the vicinity!

For the fact must be faced that nobody, not even the hardened professional, can be said to rejoice in an audience. While interest in what you are painting, or trying to paint, must be counted as flattering, it can put you off your stroke. It must never be allowed to put you off painting out of doors. I have found that you can, with practice, ignore the presence of an onlooker if you really concentrate on your work and remain deaf to any observations that are gratuitously offered. If you find this fails, you can always break off and have a pause for cleaning up. This generally acts as a hint which your spectator will take and move on. For it is not what you have painted that fascinates him, but the *act*, watching *how* you do it, that roots him to the spot. Stop performing and the act and interest are at an end.

With a companion, you can spend this interval by comparing progress and giving praise or sympathy, whichever is relevant. There is a danger, however, that if you sit sketching too close together, the casual remark can develop into a running conversation—occasional grunts, sighs or muttered expletives always excepted!

The practice of working behind your companion so that you can watch how he performs and see what is achieved may produce a pictorial astigmatism alien to a personal style and is not to be recommended. For the beginner perhaps sketching out of doors in *the company of others* is preferable to working with a single companion.

9 *Sketching Grounds*

IT has been rightly observed that it is not the business of the artist to paint what is obvious to everyone, for if it were picture post card views would, I am afraid, often be preferred to the personal impression of the cultivated mind! It is also true that one artist can extol eloquently on the pictorial charms of a locality which does not in the smallest degree affect another—or for that matter, one painter can sit down to a subject that has not the remotest appeal to other artists! Some painters prefer to work in their own country, or county, for the very reason that they know it and love it best. Others suffer from a perpetual pictorial wanderlust that drives them all over the world, to find at last their favourite setting in some remote country, where their best work will be done.

For whatever reasons artists come to be associated with different sketching grounds, it is a fatal mistake to think that by following the footsteps of a favourite painter and visiting a particular spot where this or that famous picture was painted, anyone else can do the same. Moreover, it is downright dishonest to choose the pretty and picturesque in default of a painting ground that will elevate and inspire adventure and imagination. I know too well the fascination that certain types of landscape hold for many competent amateur painters, who return to them year after year, until they are so well acquainted with the material that the actual painting becomes almost a mechanical process,

Foreign towns offer fascinating glimpses of unusual architecture.

Inland waterways afford a variety of subject matter.

foolproof in execution but moribund in artistic feeling. It is certainly obvious in their work what kind of landscape has been the cause of the formation of a particular style which has led to their downfall.

To specialise therefore in some favourite terrain can be dangerous, the favoured subject matter becoming as habit forming as a drug. Throughout the length and width of the British Isles these danger spots exist: "Low Tide—Walberswick" could well stand for the title of one of them! How well I remember the sense of exhilaration I experienced when I first saw how well this Suffolk scene and subject matter *suited my style*, and how many water colours and oils I happily painted until I realised the truth of what I have just written!

One of my paintings of Walberswick.

The same truth dawned, unwelcome I confess, but undeniable, when sketching and painting in other artists' paradises, such as Rye, Polperro, Old Shoreham and Bosham—those haunting landscapes of low horizons, mud flats, and idle fishing or yachting craft seen against a background of ancient boat houses, riverside vegetation or derelict rural habitation!

It was at such times that I "upped stakes" and sought the braver elements of the Yorkshire dales, for example, or the mountain passes of Northumberland and the Highlands, the industrial landscapes of the Midlands, and the craggy heights and valleys of Wales, for it was only a complete change of surroundings that made a change of approach essential and demanded a new technical handling of the medium. Indeed there is much to

Quarry in a Welsh valley.

be said for a fresh eye on our cities and towns, not forgetting another look at our often despised suburbs. A combination of town and country as is presented in the outskirts of London but rarely contemplated pictorially, offers a new and fruitful field for contemporary pictures. Perhaps it is not out of place here to recount the story of the late Sir Stanley Spencer, R.A., who was commissioned to paint an official picture of Plymouth. The committee took him on a tour round the city, hopefully expecting him to choose the impressive and romantic setting of the Hoe, instead of which he selected a homely subject in a side street! Unpromising material though it appeared at first sight, through Spencer's "child-like" eyes of wonder, when complete (and he took six weeks to execute it on the spot), it resulted in a painting both impressive in scope and vision—true to the last brick and flower pot and yet containing all the fundamental characteristics of this historic port. (I learnt from the curator that Spencer was never without an interested audience, mostly of children, who followed every brush stroke—and to whom he became a sort of benevolent magician.) This is surely a good example of the quotation in my introduction of "the discovery of beauty spots unmentioned in the guide books"!

10 The Camera

NO book on sketching and painting out of doors can omit mention of what I believe is becoming a growing practice with both professional and amateur alike. Certainly the how-to-do book, if not openly encouraging it, gives illustrated examples of its advantages, especially to the student or amateur who is unhandy with his pencil or is desirous of "jumping the queue" where drawing is concerned. I allude, of course, to the camera. It would appear to be taken for granted that when the sketcher goes forth to sketch, he goes armed with a camera!

There are, I agree, times and places when and where the help of a photograph is legitimate. A short pause in a journey where time is limited allowing but a passing glance at some promising subjects, is a case in point and at such times it is a blessing to be able to take a snapshot or two. Indeed, without this aid the subject might be lost, especially if a swift, but sure, impression of the scene is beyond one's technical ability. On the other hand, if the camera is always at hand—or rather in the hand—the temptation to snap the subject instead of making a sketch of it can grow to the extent of depending on it entirely for picture making. I believe it is a real danger because although in a recent book photographs of the subject were shown "as you would see the subject", this assumption is quite misleading—it is very doubtful whether you do *see* the subject like the *photograph*—but once away from Nature and with only the photograph to work from, then you tend to accept the mechanical eye of a machine, having forgotten the *impression the subject made on you*.

I know that with a well-taken photograph to work from, almost all the problems of drawing are solved, for the photograph has already translated the three-dimensional properties of the view to the two dimensions of the paper, and to some students that is a wonderful lure. But, and it's a big BUT, not only have you lost half the reward of a personal achievement in sketching from Nature, you will have lost the *personal* appeal which the subject made on you. What *you* saw *in it*, why you wanted to make a sketch or a painting of it, is lost. If you think this over, I am sure that you will only bring your camera into action when there is no time to make a careful drawing—or where detail (which is necessary to the success of your picture) may be clearly recorded in a photograph.

I would say further that the less you use a photograph, the more personal and expressive your work will become, however difficult or tiresome the technique of drawing may be found. Many years ago I had what I thought was going to be a wonderful commission from a railway company. It was for a series of drawings of various sea-side and holiday resorts, for panels in their railway carriages. I began imagining visiting all these places and finding my own subjects, only to be presented with a set of hackneyed photographs to work from! That, I think, put me off the camera for all time!

A glimpse down an unfashionable street in Nice.

11 *The Hidden View*

IT must not be forgotten that some familiar locality which as a sketching ground is thought to be pictorially worked out, can prove, on a return visit, to reveal new and unexpected subjects which before failed to catch the eye. An untrodden field path, a neglected hollow, an unpromising cul-de-sac, all of which were before unseen or unexplored, now suddenly proclaim their presence, prompting our curiosity and inviting investigation. And once again is demonstrated our blindness to much that at first failed to make a direct appeal, but which on subsequent consideration is found to be worth a sketch.

A recent experience of this kind brought the truth home to me in such a constructive fashion that I carried away half a sketch book full of fresh aspects of a village I had reluctantly dismissed as empty of any further pictures.

It also behoves one to lend an attentive ear to any friendly native who may advise an alternative route or suggest an unfamiliar vantage point from which a completely new view can be obtained. Even within the space of a dozen yards a "new look" can be given to a well-worn subject!

In the pageant of the seasons, trees denuded of their leaves can afford a clearer view of what lies behind, and hence provide a new subject. Even in detail, as can be seen with the lopping of some massive boughs from the trunk of a single tree, the new silhouette is rendered quite different in character, and what was hidden before now makes its appearance offering, perhaps, a welcome addition to the background interest.

What a complete transformation of a familiar scene can be effected by the weather! Snow, for example, and excessive rain, both act as magic wands over hitherto dull portions of the countryside. Snow, while covering up much ground interest, highlights and pinpoints all vertical forms which become brightened in colour by comparison with their whitened surroundings; while a swollen river overflowing its banks can create a series of transparent areas over erstwhile solid fields and meadows, turning arable land into a veritable lakeland.

These examples, I hope, will prove that in Nature as in human nature "good can come out of evil". I am not promising an easy sketch—on the contrary. For although the snow and the rain may have "let up", the wind, in the process of dying down, can still nip the fingers and whip the leaves of one's sketch book into a flurry of tossing paper, or worse still, rock one's easel at dangerous angles which makes accurate handling with the brush a hit or miss affair. But such climatic effects as these can only be captured at the time, and if the less adventuresome painter waits for weather conditions to improve before venturing out, the chances are that the snow will have melted, the floods subsided and all will be found as usual! I can speak with regret on both counts.

It should always be understood that if conditions prevent any further painting, as I have said elsewhere, there is still the opportunity to use your eyes and concentrate on how the elements have affected the scene. Study the change in the new colour scheme which now prevails, try to store up a visual memory of contrasting forms and colours so that, even if you return empty handed, you can try out what your eyes and mind have recorded. But whatever you bring home, don't be tempted to "dress up"

Oil Painting: Floods. Here the flooded meadows transformed a dull scene into a lively subject in which the swollen water brought colour and movement into a green and static view.

Oil Painting: Winter Landscape. The snow-covered terrain made this view pictorially possible. Note the heightened local colour on the tree trunks and distant trees enhanced by the surrounding whiteness.

your studies from Nature or tidy them up in any way, for such considered touches that you introduce will rarely harmonise with the gestures your brush has dictated while painting with that degree of urgency prompted by the mood of the moment. More than half the value of your sketch lies in its spontaneity—its "unscripted" handling. Remember, too, that the process of enlarging your sketch to the size of a finished picture must be consistent in technique from start to finish. If this produces a somewhat different appeal to that of your original sketch, it will nevertheless have in common the virtue of pictorial truth.

An unfamiliar vantage-point gives a new look.

(Private collection.)

In this painting I asked the boys to pose for a deliberate composition in which I used the boat to link up the design.

12 *Figures*

FIGURES naturally play an important part in many out of door paintings, especially in street scenes, and care must be taken to introduce them where a focal point is needed and not always where they happen to be! Yet—and this is the difficulty—for the device to be successful, the figures should never appear to be posed, but, as in the words above, "where they happen to be"! I have given examples of right and wrong placing.

As a general rule, figures should be *found*, rather than force their attention upon us. There are many serviceable symbols (for the beginner) which can be used and varied according to need.

Back and front views are preferable to side view, and figures in action, walking or running, should be avoided. Their pictorial value is to introduce life in the form of "animated repose" into any scene in which the human element is usually found and without which the subject appears deserted. The same rules also apply to animals—sheep, horses or cattle—wherever they occur in open landscapes. In a word, both human beings and animals should "dress" the scene, but never dominate it, unless of course the subject is a figure or animal composition, when the procedure is reversed and the setting remains subordinate in interest to the human or animal forms.

Incidentally Constable, that inveterate painter out of doors, was once quoted as saying with regard to some landscape where a heron had been introduced, "Yes, I saw it, I had sat a long time without a living thing making its appearance. I always sit till I see some living thing, because if any such appears, it is sure to be appropriate to a place. If no living object shows itself, I put none in to my picture."

A better known example of his desire for truth is seen in the number of sky studies in oils with notes on the back of time of day, and direction of wind.

The road slopes steeply at A—the eye is level with the horizon line—hence parallel lines, i.e. roofs, windows, etc., of the cottages will all slant upwards. *I have underlined these.*

13 Perspective

ENCOURAGING and optimistic as one longs to be, a warning here must not be overlooked. It is that a working knowledge of perspective is not only expedient but a vital necessity when sketching many subjects out of doors. It will always come to one's aid when architectural forms are found in Nature. After all there are many views which include man-made objects, like walls, fences, barns, houses and churches, and frequently these are seen in recession! Occasionally they follow a road which either ascends or descends from the position you wish to make your sketch.

The examples I have given are often neglected or avoided (shunned is Augustus John's word) because of the apparent difficulty of representing the steepness of the road, whether it goes up or down. To achieve the illusion of looking down,

St. Ives, Cornwall. Note the direction of the various arrow-heads.

which is the harder of the two, the greatest care must be taken in following faithfully the upward direction of all the lines of roof and window ledges that occur in the scene. In the illustration (p. 64) I have underlined those that slant upwards because it is only by this means that the spectator will realise that he is *looking down with you* on the subject. The steeper the hill, the higher the horizon line must be, and the steeper the slant upwards of the roofs, etc.

In previous books in this series I have attempted to exorcise the bogey of perspective. If the simple rules have been properly understood, and the eye is trained to distinguish between lines that go across and those that go up or down, then the sloping or rising contours of the terrain will cease to be a menace, however steep the ascent or descent happens to be.

I do not say that this is so in all cases, but there are some views where half the charm will be lost if by default the subject matter

You are looking down *at the boats and the river. The outline of the stone balustrade must ascend steeply, otherwise the effect of looking down will be lost.*

St. Ives, Cornwall. The effect of looking up is established by the slant of the roofs, A, *and the borders of the alley way,* B.

is represented on the level when it is meant to be viewed from above or below!

An art mistress whom I was recently questioning on this controversial subject said she never taught perspective as the few children who continued their art (or took it up professionally) would never feel the need of it. But surely the answer is that only a knowledge of perspective can determine its value or not in their picture making. After all, it is not an artificial device—everybody, whether they can draw or not, *sees* everything in perspective: it is only a matter of teaching the hand to follow the eye.

On the other hand, every artist is free to use it or not. It has certainly never been considered indispensable to a work of art and may even prove obsolete as time goes on and representative painting is given up in favour of non-representational art.

In the meantime and especially when painting out of doors is still practised, perspective, like other pictorial first aid devices, can heal a sickly piece of drawing and greatly strengthen a weakly painting.

14 *The Personal Approach*

TO achieve complete independence in approach and technical handling should be the ultimate aim of all students, whether they are producing pictures in the studio or painting direct from Nature. I repeat "ultimate", because for some time striving to achieve "realistic truth" ("to make it *like*") is as much as the student can usually manage! In the end, however, the reward comes and a purely personal statement may be permitted. The desire to express oneself must then not be weakened by any fear that the means employed may appear unorthodox—or "modern"!

To illustrate this I have chosen a recent painting (see opposite) which I executed in the South of France—*on the spot*. Whether the result will be found favourable to all readers is beside the point. All I can hope for is that if the reasons appear acceptable for adopting this style, the result should be admitted as justifying the means employed. I decided that this subject, if rendered conventionally, that is, in the traditional manner, would not (to me) have been worth the painting. At the same time, I began to see in it something pictorial that prompted an increasing urge to express what I *felt*. As I sat in contemplation, this "something" that would epitomise the subject matter suddenly resolved itself in terms of evocative symbols—which, if successful, would offer sufficient clues for the beholder to fill in the gaps and thereby finish the picture. This resolve necessitated quick action; to hesitate over the amount of preliminary drawing required would

Watercolour painting of Cap Ferrat. (In the possession of Miss Evelyn Hardy.)

have been fatal. So I merely drew in with my carbon pencil the absolute essentials—the angle and silhouette of the central tree—the slant of the rocks—the outline of the coastline. A sort of wire cage, in fact, which would support the weight of the subsequent painting. With a brush full of Prussian blue diluted with water, I painted round the trees on the headland, carrying the wash of colour outwards, and left the margins, as will be seen, with a vignetted outline, which with bold economy would, I decided, suffice to suggest both sky and encroaching clouds. To balance both colour and shape of this sky portion, I proceeded to lay in the sea with pure Prussian blue. By adopting a similar serrated outline, I suggested movement while taking the eye back to the rocky coast.

With brown madder I filled in the rugged stem of the pine tree, and diluting this colour with water I washed in certain areas of the cliff face. The vegetation, which was prolific, was sparingly suggested so as not to overweigh the preceding colours.

I do not suppose that the whole thing took longer than twenty minutes to complete. And if "complete" may appear paradoxical in view of the amount of unpainted paper in the sketch, I hope it will be seen that no further filling in could achieve any artistic purpose, but would rather rob the story of its point.

Finish, it must always be remembered, comes at that particular moment when any additional information will confuse the very legibility of the communication. I know just how tempting it is with a brush hovering over your picture to add some explanatory touch or two, and having once begun to tidy up, how difficult it is to know when to desist from helping the spectator. For the beholder, as Ruskin puts it, must be allowed to follow out his own thoughts, "The artist is his conveyance, not his companion —his horse, not his friend."

15 *Another Kind of Approach*

IN contrast to the approach, form and colour of the sketch discussed in the last chapter, I want to tell you how the painting on the next page came into being.

There are, you will find, various causes which influence both subject and mood, together with circumstance and environment, all of which make an oblique impact on how the painter performs. Why he sees it as he does may even be a matter of health! Call it a whim, a conceit, a resolution, or even an answer to a self-imposed challenge—whatever it may be, it is this sudden and sometimes unexplained directive that decides the manner of the painting.

This typical harbour scene at Beaulieu on the Côte D'Azur, came under review as the car slowed down on my route along the coast road to Italy. It was midday and I wanted to stretch my legs. Gathering up my painting materials and leaving my travelling companions on the promenade, I made my way down the harbour steps to the water level. No sooner was I there than I decided to make a sketch, and without further delay I sat down and immediately started on making a brief chalk indication of the composition. While thus engaged I wondered, just for a moment, why I was content to execute the painting, as I knew I would, in the same way or style as I had done on innumerable occasions in the past.

The answer came from above my head! My companions were sitting on the parapet watching the performance, and for this

Watercolour painting of the Harbour, Beaulieu.

reason I made up my mind I would "toe the party line" and paint my sketch in the approved fashion, the only difference being that it would be better than any past painting executed in the accepted terms of watercolour. This dubious resolve was made easier to carry out because I knew in advance all the little technical difficulties and how to overcome—or evade—them! I couldn't afford to make a failure and time was a pressing factor. Considering all these things, the charge of "playing for safety" did not worry me, and I had no conscience in the risk I took of painting "just another watercolour".

In the end speed alone came to my rescue, when wholesale simplifications had to be made, especially in the windows of the houses and in the clutter of fishing craft in the harbour basin. In both instances a more leisurely notation would have sealed the fate of my painting's very life, and if this has been retained it is only because I knew when to take a chance with a fully loaded brush, where to apply it, and how to refrain from tidying up the results.

My friendly but critical audience, I am glad to record, were unanimous in their agreement that I had hit off the scene. "Hit off" perhaps is the right expression in this case!

Conclusion

TO sum up. Painting direct from Nature to the majority of painters remains a means—and to many, an indispensable means—to an end, but not an end in itself. That I feel must be acknowledged, however devoted we are to Nature and in whatever degree of reverence we worship at her shrine, as some of us are content to do.

As Nature is always over-lavish with her wares, so they must be considered as "raw" material to be "made up" according to our own requirements. By sketching and painting out of doors we are invited to inspect the material at close quarters, to handle, as it were, and judge for ourselves its quality, texture and durability. The choice is ours: what we do with it is our responsibility. When I confess, as I have done on many occasions, that "I am never happier than when I'm painting out of doors", I always add "except when I'm painting in my studio"!

Finally, if we are really interested in finding out what Nature has still to offer, then Nature will still remain our true and inexhaustible source of supply, the fountain head from which our own personal paintings are nourished and brought to fruition.

Index

Other Books by Adrian Hill

WHAT SHALL WE DRAW?

"In this book, as in television programmes, Adrian Hill stimulates the reader in more than just desire for craftsmanship. He asks us to see things as they really are, and then to portray them. In easy style and clear steps, the book unfolds some of the fundamental stages in sketching."—*Health Education Journal*

THE BEGINNER'S BOOK OF OIL PAINTING

"A very practical approach to the subject by a master of the craft. .... Throughout this book the reader is encouraged to be himself and to try his own experiment. . . ."—*The Schoolmaster*

THE BEGINNER'S BOOK OF WATERCOLOUR PAINTING

"The information given, whether it concerns brushes, colours, equipment or technique, is always absolutely sound, as is his insistence on a personal approach. The illustrations are a joy."

The Schoolmaster

KNOWING AND DRAWING TREES, Books 1 and 2

"Anyone with an appreciation of natural beauty will find this small though beautifully produced volume a delight to possess. Adrian Hill has the technical skill of a first-rate draughtsman plus the selective perception and good taste of a first-rate artist."

Art News and Review

FACES AND FIGURES

"Full of extremely valuable practical hints to the aspiring craftsman, and the text is embellished by excellent illustrations and diagrams."

London Head Teacher

SKETCHING AND PAINTING INDOORS

"This is the sort of book which immediately sends the young artist to his sketch book."—*Art and Craft Education*

ADVENTURES IN PAINTING

The story of BBC "Sketch Club" with over 100 (46 in full colour) reproductions of prize-winning entries.